First United States edition published in 1996 by Barron's Educational Series, Inc.
Copyright © 1995 by Casterman sa Tournai, Belgium.
The title of the original edition is *Bouquets des Peintres.*

Translation from the French by Annie Heminway.

All inquiries should be addressed to:
Barron's Educational Series, Inc.
250 Wireless Boulevard
Hauppauge, New York 11788

All flower arrangements created by
CATLEYA
118, av. Louis-Lepoutre
1060 Brussels

Graphic concept

Nicolas Gilson

Decoration

Luc Chaufoureau

Vases

Private collection of Mr. and Mrs. Van de Putte
The publishers wish to thank the Habitat Group and
Mr. José Roland for their assistance

Historical adviser

Lillo Canta

•

Photo credits
pages 16, 18, 37
Giraudon

page 31
Scala

pages 51, 57
Bridgeman-Giraudon

pages 43, 69
AKG, Berlin

page 81
Christie's · AKG, Berlin

pages 19, 24, 63, 75, 87, 93
Lauros-Giraudon

page 99
© Succession Henri Matisse · Photo AKG, Berlin

page 105
© Sabam Bruxelles 1995 · Photo Scala

page 111
© Sabam, Bruxelles, 1995
Thyssen-Bornemisza Collection Foundation, Madrid 1994

Library of Congress Catalog Card Number 95-83244
International Standard Book Number 0-8120-6578-6

PRINTED IN SPAIN

6789   7150   987654321

BOUQUETS

Floral Arrangements

of the Masters

BOUQUETS
BRIGITTE FUX

PHOTOGRAPHS
ZVONOK

Roots

It is said that everything began in a garden. In this garden, there was fresh, cool water, as well as luscious fruits, and flowers that were splendid but useless. It was not because they had medicinal properties that flowers were so important in this wondrous place. It was their colors, their shapes, their fragrance, and their singular charm. Flowers remind us that beauty lasts for only a fragile moment; their mystery is due to their ephemeral quality. They have the nostalgic fragrance of a paradise lost. Through their forms and colors, flowers are symbols—more than any other natural element. Through the centuries, a rich and universal language of flowers has developed. Its grammar has evolved with civilization's mentality and morals, each culture progressively enriching it. For instance, in the Western world, red roses declare the ardent passion of first love; chrysanthemums are reminders of those who have died; white lilies are offered as a pledge of devotion to the Immaculate Conception. Other species play a similar role in South America or Asia—their attributes are numerous and generally positive. A gift of flowers almost always indicates a bond. At the beginning of a relationship, flowers are a bouquet of love; at its twilight, a funeral wreath. Well before the beginning of history, flowers enchanted human beings. Their blossoming during the Neolithic spring was probably greeted as a festival celebrating the return of sunny days and mild weather. Edible plants, herbal medicines, pigments, pollens, and perfumes were discovered very early in human history. They were greatly valued for personal ornament, and perhaps were even offered in tributes.

Lotus (*Lotus*)

Flowers from the Gods

It is not surprising that biblical people considered the precious oasis, with its shade and coolness, a metaphor for the Garden of Eden, the supreme ideal of human happiness. From the Mediterranean Basin to the Far East, gardens held an important place in the ancient system of symbols. Fruits, garlands, wreaths, and bouquets were offered to the gods, gradually replacing bloody sacrifices. The Near East is rich in sculptures that represented kings or gods holding a lotus flower or a palm leaf. In a religious context, flowers and plants, both real or symbolic, celebrated life while emphasizing its fragility. Examples are the delicate frescoes that decorate the tombs in the Nile Valley. In Thebes, sheaves of flowers crowned the opulent offering tables. The same scenes appeared in Knossos or in Etruria. The decorative power of flowers was widely used by ancient people. Stylized garlands were sculpted in bas-relief on the walls of Mesopotamian towns.

In Babylon, the Hanging Gardens, offered by Nebuchadnezzar II to Amytis, his love, are considered one of the wonders of the world. The same designs appear on clothes and rugs. The lotus flower is the most widely used motif in the Orient because, as an aquatic symbol, it is believed to ward off fire. The capitals of the Assyrian, Phoenician, or Egyptian temples copied its corolla. Waterlilies, crocuses, carnations, and daisies blossomed on the geometric motifs of Greek and Cretan vases.

Lotus fruit (*Lotus*)

An Unadorned God

Of all the people who created beautiful floral ensembles in the Fertile Crescent, the tribes of Israel were the only exception. Jews worshipped only one God, Yahweh, Creator of Heaven and Earth. He did not appear in person to his people, avoiding their gazing directly upon him. Nor did he allow them to capture him in an image or statue. For the God of the Scriptures and the Word, only prayer is real, images being mere illusions. And, by extension, all that the eye can see, appearance or seduction, is sin and therefore forbidden. Even today, Orthodox Jewish synagogues are almost totally devoid of decoration. No vegetation and absolutely no flowers are found in Orthodox Jewish cemeteries. Instead, pebbles are placed on the headstones of the graves by visitors paying their respects. This rejection of icons would heavily influence the future of images, and thus the future of flowers.

Oak leaves (*Quercus*)

Latin Roses

The first paintings where flowers were featured as a major motif were in ancient Rome. Daisies, roses, sweetbrier, violets, crocuses, gladioli, lilies, and myrtle decorated the frescoes that surrounded the *horti*, dramatically enlarging these small city gardens. On sanctuary walls in Pompeii, Stabies, or Herculanum, the *lararium,* a wreath painted in trompe l'oeil, immortalized the offering, which thus became permanent. Purists regarded this novelty with suspicion. Offering artificial flowers was not appreciated in the ancient world, as it is still not today. But the introduction of floral presentations can be explained by the role that the luxury products played in Roman society. Although, at first, wreaths rewarded the courage of warriors or the skill of athletes, in the second century, under the Roman Empire, this practice was trivialized. Not only flowers, but also exotic fruits, perfumes, ointments, spices, jewels, and fabrics were the ostentatious symbols of social status. They were reserved for those who could afford them.

Thanks to sophisticated horticultural techniques, the quality of flowers improved. The prosperity and refinement achieved by Rome at its height would not be equaled for a long time. From the third century on, the Roman Empire underwent its agonizing decline—a litany of domestic upheavals, incessant parceling out of the land, and barbarian invasions. A long winter followed the fall of the Roman Empire. Even if newcomers adopted certain aspects of the Roman way of life, the extremely difficult economic conditions no longer permitted luxury and pleasure. Agricultural techniques and botanical skills were inexorably lost. Numerous varieties of plants, fruits, and vegetables, once the pride of patrician tables, disappeared for a long time. The ancient displays of splendor were revived in Byzantium, the gateway to the East, which carefully preserved its Greek and Roman heritage. It is through this gate, after many years, that a great part of the classical heritage was rediscovered by the West.

Mulberry tree (*Morusnigra*)

Forbidden Flowers

Of all the revolutions that shook the declining Roman Empire, the most fundamental was the new religion, Christianity. Monotheists and egalitarians, who rejected the cult of idols and emperors, the early Christians were first persecuted before their faith spread throughout the continent. Austerity and Puritanism characterized the dawn of Christianity. The church fathers, spiritual guides to the faithful, repeated the Jewish anathema, battling against the pagan heritage and its rites, idolatry, and the creation of false deities. Wreaths of flowers decorating the statues of the gods were banned, as they mocked the crown of thorns worn by the sacrificed Christ. Christians fought against the pagan conception of life that celebrated nature and its representation for the benefit of a more abstract, transcendental, and immaterial religiosity.

However, the attempts to erase paganism collided with a strong popular resistance, especially in the countryside. Heretical beliefs reappeared continuously, integrated in the new rituals by the faithful. Seeking to purge worship of the Golden Calf, paganism reappeared in new forms. The rejection of idols was not universal. Some of the most prestigious Christian thinkers believed that images played an educational role for an illiterate public lacking direct contact with the Scriptures, and they therefore encouraged the creation and diffusion of icons. Often excluded from sanctuaries, images were tolerated nearby, as long as they were used only for decoration. To offset the too obvious nudity of forbidden statues, "flat images" (notably frescoes) were born. These "divine" figures, elegantly stylized, floated in a space of gold. Closer to the spiritual ideal, they were more readily accepted than sculptured images. This symbolic representation of nature—extraordinarily aesthetic—is inadequate, however, for effectively producing accurate botanical studies, which depend upon a precise and realistic visualization. Far from being innocent or marginal, the attitude toward icons led to fundamental debate within the new religion. Its accessibility to the world and vulgarization were in question. The bloody "battle of images" placed the supporters of icons and their enemies, the "iconoclasts," in bitter opposition. This civil war, which tore apart the Eastern Church was not theologically resolved until 787. The Second Council of Nicea established the legitimacy of the cult of images, but did not put an end to the controversy.

Moorish Paradise

Islam, which dominated the world from Spain to Persia beginning in the seventh and eighth centuries, was much stricter in banning images but more tolerant concerning certain other decoration. Not permitted to paint human and animal forms, artists turned to flowers and calligraphy. Persian rugs—products of the meeting of the Arab and Eastern world—held a privileged place among all artistic creations. Their motifs reproduced the cruciform plan of a Muslim garden, surrounded by floral borders. The paradise garden was almost the exclusive domain of the rose, which also played a key role in Arab literature. Poets composed anthologies of poems to its glory with verses linked like flowers in a garland. Medieval Europe later imported this tradition and created the "florilegium," the anthology of verse.

The Country of Chrysanthemums and Bamboo

From ancient times, the production and the role of flowers have been more important in China than elsewhere because of a particularly favorable climate and the mastery of intensive agricultural techniques. These techniques, advanced for their time, were developed in rice fields and tea plantations. Adept at hybridization, the Chinese created a large variety of flowers that appeared in Europe much later: chrysanthemums, wisteria, gardenias, orchids, and innumerable species of roses. A number of flowering trees also have Chinese origins, like the magnolia and the camellia. Certain varieties of fruit trees (cherry, peach) were singled out because of the beauty of their blossoms. The Chinese also developed a complex pharmacology based on the study of medicinal plants. The arrival of Buddhism in China introduced the idea of nature on a human scale. This domesticated conception of the universe is perfectly represented in the bonsai of gardeners who specialized in miniature gardens. From the fifth century on, as cities grew in both China and Japan, the garden became increasingly important. It offered, in the heart of the city, an atmosphere of calm and rest, unadorned and minimalist, and conducive to meditation. The same spirit rules the *ikebana*, the art of Japanese floral arrangement. Triggered by the invention of paper (third century B.C.), painting and calligraphy rapidly developed. Drawing and writing, practiced with the same instrument—the paint brush—were intertwined. In court poems, the drawings of flowers and ideograms were closely intertwined, like the orchid and the bamboo, reinforcing the eternal metaphor of feminine charm and floral grace. The academies that taught floral drawing and landscape composition also published manuals that presented the principal floral models. Craft artists found there some motifs that they applied to silverwork, porcelain, or silk.

A Thousand Woven Flowers

Before the twelfth century, Europe lived in slow motion, at the edge of the great economic and intellectual currents that flowed across the world, from the Near East to the Far East. Their floral culture was rudimentary, compared to what was happening in China or Turkey. The monks piously preserved the knowledge of the ancient world and its Byzantine resurgence. In the heart of cloisters, in monastic gardens, vegetables, vines, fruit trees, and medicinal herbs were grown. In the Middle Ages, the salvation of the soul and the body were intertwined. Some flowers were grown to decorate the altar on special occasions. But science did not make any real progress and the few botanical treatises in circulation were copies from the ancient world.

Outside the monastic boundaries, the first decorative orchards provided the setting for knightly jousts. They looked like mythical gardens enclosed by arbors of climbing roses that protected the virginal purity of Mary. The favorite flower of classic poets, and the voluptuous image of carnal love, the rose was transformed into a Marian sign. In *Le Roman de la Rose (The Tale of the Rose)*, the conquest of the flower symbolized the quest for the absolute ideal. The walls of feudal dwellings were decorated with rich hangings called *millefleurs* (a thousand flowers). A meadow strewn with easily identifiable species (roses, lilies, gladioli, hyacinths, broom, columbines, violets, poppies, pansies, peonies) decorated the scenes—religious and profane—illustrated by weavers. In the countryside, popular wisdom perpetuated ancient knowledge. Peasants spread the secrets of plants, roots, and flowers from generation to generation. They knew how to extract fibers for weaving from hemp and flax, drawing very useful blue or red dyes from woad (an herb in the mustard family) or madder (an herb with red roots). Mandrake juice calmed their fevers and eased their coughs. Lavender oil relieved their nervous ailments. The ancient pagan beliefs persisted and evolved. Upon the arrival of spring in the villages, people crowned virtuous young girls with white roses, converting an ancient pagan ceremony into the benefit of the cult of Mary.

A Renaissance in the Margins of Books

The Western history of flower painting was reborn in the margin of books. If the first manuscripts were devoid of images, ornate letters or abstract motifs appeared in the English and Irish liturgical manuals between the sixth and seventh centuries, in response to an old tradition of filling any empty spaces. That "distaste for the blank space," is at the origin of the creation of a rich repertoire of tracery and geometric forms (particularly among the Celts and Germans). Little by little, the monks-copyists meticulously framed the sacred texts with botanical representations based on the model of borders used to decorate Oriental rugs. The rejection of illustrations in the margins of manuscripts was not a gratuitous act; it perfectly illustrated their still ambiguous status. But this mistrust was not universal. Southern Europe, profoundly influenced by ancient Rome, remained in the classical tradition. Its people were more sensitive to images and flowers. From the year 1000, first bas-reliefs, then sculptures, made their appearance in the Roman Catholic churches, along with a number of other liturgical objects, such as: candelabras, baptismal fonts, and reliquaries. The plant designs brought some of the outside world into the church, marking the eternal cycle of the seasons. The evangelization and pilgrimages generated a new set of didactic material and led to the illustration of biblical stories. In these manuscripts, decorated borders were given more and more space, progressively occupying the center of the page. The twelfth-century Gothic cathedrals, filled with sculptures and stained glass windows, marked the definite return of the figurative that triumphed in the thirteenth century with the Italian Renaissance.

If Giotto and Cimabue's masterpieces still owe much to the Byzantine icons, which surfaced after the taking of Constantinople by the Crusaders in 1204, they also marked a fundamental departure—the return of nature in art. Saint Francis of Assisi and Thomas Aquinas offered a new and immense

Chrysanthemum (*Chrysanthemum*)

**Flowered margins in the missal
of Jean de Lannoy (fifteenth
century), Municipal Library,
Lille, France.**

repertoire of models that celebrated the beauty of nature, reflecting the grandeur of the Creator. To faithfully reproduce the world in order to create the illusion of reality was the credo that obsessed artists from then on.

Sacred Birth

Artists were essentially inspired by biblical history. If a large number of bouquets (which have, in current usage, supplanted garlands), expanded beyond the altar, their presence remained strictly secondary to religious symbolism. Flowers, which were used in holy processions, certainly had a decorative function relative to the talent of the artist, but their principal role was to transmit a clearly decipherable doctrinal message. Thus, the garland of roses that surrounded the Virgin Mary in many fifteenth-century portraits evoked the purity of her love if they were white and the sacrifice of her son if bloodred. This is an evolution of floral borders proper to manuscripts. The innovators—Jan van Eyck, Hans Memling, Hugo van der Goes, Le Maître de Flémalle—liberated them from these constraints.

Pitchers, vases, and pots filled with bouquets of flowers appeared in windows or on the steps of the altar. These sites were more realistic, conforming to the common usage of the time, but they also played a role in the composition. The bouquets contributed to the definition of pictorial space in perspective, putting an emphasis on the foreground, underlining the direction. Certainly, the vase of flowers was still not considered worthy of being represented by itself if it was not used as an overleaf of a panel or to play a secondary role in the decoration of furniture. By the end of the century, the illuminators of the schools of Bruges and Ghent brought to life page margins with a multitude of flowers. The meticulous detail foreshadowed the scientific illustrations of the centuries to come. The custom of placing everyday objects in paintings became widespread, until their presence, at first needed to denote realism and to specify religious meaning, became a handicap. Starting in Holland in the middle of the sixteenth century, a number of biblical portrayals of domestic scenes became a pretext for magnifying daily life. It is true that, in the meantime, socioeconomic conditions had radically changed. A new social class had appeared, the bourgeoisie (middle class)— Protestants in Holland and Catholics in Flanders. Gradually, merchants replaced the church in commissioning works of art. These *nouveaux riches* (newly rich) sought images that reflected their way of life, adding to the decor of their homes. They chose the new pictorial genres: the portrait, a faithful mirror of the triumphant bourgeois; the landscape, his property; and the still life, items from his pantry. The size of the paintings decreased in order to adapt to the size of the homes, which were much smaller than the grand palaces and churches.

A Passion for Botany

In this context, flowers took on a very special value. People suddenly had a passion for curio cabinets. The first botanical gardens minutely preserved exotic plants arriving from the newly discovered territories: sunflowers, balsam, tulips, lemon balm, agaves, sweetbrier, mandrake, marigolds, poppies, and so on.

Solomon's seal (*Polygonatum*)

Early flower vases, center panel of the Portinari triptych, around 1479, by Hugo van der Goes, Uffizzi Gallery, Florence, Italy.

The men who were part of the Renaissance were steeped in classical learning, curious about everything, informed, thanks to the printing press (illustrated scientific works began to proliferate), obsessed about labeling, classifying, organizing, and exploring the universe, and armed with revolutionary tools such as the magnifying glass (soon to be followed by the microscope). They passionately loved flowers because they evoked sweetness (honey was the only sweetener then known), for their perfume (successive hybrids had not yet weakened their fragrances), and especially for their value. Indeed, some hyacinth or tulip bulbs could cost astronomical sums. Their commerce unleashed frenzies like the "tulipmania."

Tulip Madness

Introduced in Europe by Ghislain de Busbecq, ambassador of Ferdinand of Austria to Istanbul, the tulip—the Turkish *tülbend* (turban)—arrived in Holland in 1578. The Dutch adopted the newcomer with great enthusiasm that has not diminished to this day. The watery terrain was favorable for its growth, and the horticulturists proved to be very successful at creating new species through hybridization. The tulip trade prospered to such a degree that bulbs were soon listed on the Stock Exchange. Sometimes, the merchants used illustrations of flowering tulips to help buyers decide on their purchase, as they could only trade in bulbs before they flowered.

A frenzied speculation exploded, fed by increasing demand, the whims of fashion, and the unpredictability of new colors. Tulip fever struck across class lines. In February, 1637, prices collapsed, triggering an unprecedented stock market crash and causing a rash of bankruptcies. Tulipmania was the first serious stock market crisis. Capitalism, which was just developing, reacted by severely regulating the market.

One trend led to another. Paintings of flowers proliferated on the moldings of cornices of bourgeois homes in Holland. These images went beyond being decorative. Today, they would be considered status symbols. The interest in progress and especially money was proudly flaunted. In reality, the bouquets represented were impossible to assemble. Species that blossomed at different times of the year were presented together, displayed according to their best angle without concern for accuracy, and distorting the length of their stems. These paintings were plant illustrations. We can imagine the owners showing off their knowledge, commenting before their guests about the new species: tulips, hyacinths, anemones, crocuses, irises, carnations, fritillaria. These images had other advantages. They substituted for rare and unaffordable flowers. Some spotted tulips or the celebrated "sky blues" cost far more than the work of artists. The painting guaranteed the owners a permanence that, unfortunately, real flowers lacked. These artists prospered in Flanders and The Netherlands, including the masters, Jan Brueghel, also called de Velours, who was the most celebrated of all, Lodewijck van den Bosch,

Tulip (*Tulipa*)

Ambrosius Bosschaert, Roelandt Savery, Osias Beert, Abraham Mignon, Carel Van Mander, Jan Baers, Jacon de Gheyn, and Daniel Seghers. In Paris, Jacques Linard, Lubin Baugin, and others begin painting flowers with enthusiasm, while in Spain, Blas de Lesdema, Zubarán, and Sanchez Cotán gave to their *bodegones* (still lifes) a majestic austerity. Protestant Germany welcomed a number of refugees fleeing religious intolerance: Georg Flegel, Peter Binoit, Joris Hoefnagel, and Sébastian Stokkopff, who faithfully reproduced the Dutch style. Meanwhile, Italians—except for the ancient *grotteschi*, (associating nature with monsters)—and some fragments of Carvaggio, seemed to pay less attention to painted bouquets, preferring set tables.

Creating of a Genre

Not every still life celebrated the triumph of money. The seventeenth century was also the century of religious reforms and counter-reforms. It marked the return of morality. For the Protestant, as well as the Catholic, meditation about death was an essential spiritual exercise. And, like doubt gradually seeping in, new characters quietly made their appearance in the small pictures that until then had been strictly regulated. Beetles, snails, dragonflies, and lizards insinuated themselves into the midst of this lushness. Sometimes an overripe tulip or rose with its petals drooping appeared. At the foot of the vases lay broken petals. Elsewhere, the empty sockets of skulls emerged from the shadows. The hourglass and the clock proclaimed the march of time; the knowledge contained in the books and the precision of instruments cannot stop its movement. These details, reminding the viewer of the vanity of all mortal things, are the subject of the paintings of Jan Davidsz de Heem, Pieter Claesz, Pieter Potter, Willem Claesz Heda, and Gerard Dou. Unbalanced presentations, astutely designed bouquets with rough contours, the buzzing of insects, curves, arches, and complex meanings—flower painting seemed like an autonomous pictorial genre and not a substitute for a still life.

It was at that time that the first flower vases arrived from China, receptacles specifically designed to contain flowers that had formerly been placed in jugs or pots.

The vases were part of the porcelain imported in large quantities from China. The floral motifs that decorated them profoundly influenced European production, most notably the blue porcelain of Delft. A comparable event took place with Indian cotton. Colored and floral calicoes were an immediate success, so successful that some tried to restrict their importation in order to protect local industries. European artisans soon adapted and adopted Oriental motifs. Plates, cushions, quilts, and walls were covered with flowers.

Perfumes from Other Lands

In the seventeenth century, exoticism was in fashion. One of the first thing explorers did when arriving in unknown territory was to inventory the native flora and fauna. On their return, the novelties found their way to the most sumptuous and extravagant feasts. It is in this manner that the passionflower arrived from America (Christianized by the missionaries), along with tomatoes, corn, potatoes, and cocoa beans. Asia sent its share of novelties: orchids, camellias, wisteria, forsythia, carnations, asters, lupine, and phlox. Orange

orchards and greenhouses were built to insure the permanent presence of fruits and exotic flowers at the best tables.

The botanist painters became floral artists. Their canvases became fuller, the arrangements more complex, and everyday objects gave way to precious instruments and prestigious accessories. At the same time that the still life was ennobled, it reached the halls of the royal palace. Jean-Baptiste Monnoyer and Jean-Baptise Blin de Fontenay worked at the court of Louis XIV. In Italy, Mario and Guiseppe Recco, Mario Nuzzi dei Fiori, Andrea Belvedere, Gaspare Lopez, Peirano Genovese, Gian Battista Ruopollo, Giovanna Garzoni, and Luca Forte frequented the palaces of the Neopolitan, Roman, and Turinian princes. At the same time, the Spanish Juan de Arellano, Gabriel de la Corte, and Bartoleme Pérez, and the Dutch Nicolas van Veerendael, Pieter Jan Frans van Son, Jacob van Walscapelle, Pieter van Loo, and Pieter Holstyen were faced with the same phenomenon.

Assembly Line Bouquets

In the eighteenth century, the progressive transition from mercantile capitalism to industrial capitalism triggered a radical evolution of the market. Rare commodities, once reserved for the rich, were produced mechanically in larger numbers and at lower costs. This was the case with cotton prints and wallpaper, which replaced hand-manufactured products. Most were decorated with flowers. Thanks to the progress of printing, the first botanical books intended for a relatively large audience were published. The courts of Europe had a passion for flowers. After the Revolution in France, the king's garden was converted into a museum of natural history. The empress Josephine commissioned rare vellum editions from Pierre-Joseph Redouté, her teacher of floral design. In turn, these drawings influenced artisans, encouraging the rebirth of fabrics, tapestries, embroideries, porcelain, and gold work.

Seed catalogs were printed and widely circulated. They encouraged a general taste for flowers that had been primarily restricted, until then, to the cities. Authorities encouraged people to grow gardens, in part to insure basic subsistence for families, but also, in this era of utopian socialism, for their great educational value. Following Rousseau, gardening became a fashionable trend. Amateur gardeners grew in number. This was especially true in England, which had inherited its passion for flowers from neighboring Holland. In this area, the British supremacy cannot be denied. The range of new flowers continued to increase: hydrangeas, sweet peas, dahlias, wisteria, chrysanthemums, fuchsias, fritillaria, gladioli, marigolds, and azaleas. In 250 years, botany was enriched by more than 20,000 new species, which led to some confusion among plant illustrators. The Swede Carl von Linnaeus developed a new classification to rationally organize the evolution of botanical knowledge. For artists, the bouquet offered the opportunity to display their virtuosity. They first adopted a baroque, then a rococo style. The compositions were astounding and convoluted; colors became hard and cold; forms strived for perfection. The style was refined, but it lost in spontaneity what it gained in virtuosity. Paul Theodor van Brussel, Rachel Ruysch, Willem van der Aelst, Jan Van Huysum, Gerard van Spaendonck, Jan Franz van Dael, and Jan and Georgius van Os led this new age of artistic devotion. At the fringe of official art, illustrators, who created models for the factories, sometimes added emotion to their simple designs.

City Flowers

The cut flower market was born in the nineteenth century, when the custom of having fresh flowers in the house or offering a bouquet as a gift started to spread. It was dominated by Holland (and still is). From the initial stages of the production, growers established professional societies that organized the first floral exhibitions. In the marketplaces and on the sidewalks, the young, charming, strolling flower girl became a fixture on the urban scene. She earned respectability by setting up stalls, then opening posh stores. In 1819 Charlotte de Latour published the *ABC's of Flowers,* which gave precise meaning to *selams* (the name given to the bouquets that contained a message). This dictionary defined the colors, the selection of fragrances, and the arrangement of flowers. It drew on ancient mythology as well as poems (such as *La guirlande de Julie, [Julie's Garland],* a collection of madrigals illustrated by Nicolas Robert in 1653), in order to expound on the associations of flowers and their meanings: violets and modesty, roses and passion, lilies and purity, ivy and faithfulness, forget-me-nots and true love—tenacious clichés that still remain with us today.

Contempt for the Academy

The art world ignored flowers. In the academies, pomposity triumphed. Artists placed great emphasis on sweeping, neoclassic, mythological scenes and historic reenactments. Landscapes and still lifes were ignored, considered insignificant, even vulgar, unworthy of being included on the walls of the salons. Flowers were not to be seen again on canvases until the Impressionists. The ideals of "sublime" beauty and truth returned, remaining until the nineteenth century in France. But the Academy became frozen in its contemplation of the past. Teaching was provided by an honorary corps of artists named for life, who tyrannically ruled over the creative process. They imposed their style and controlled the examinations, the marketplace, and any artistic creations. The artists exhibited their works during the social event of the year, the Salon, considered the only "proper" place to appreciate art at that time. Artists were given the honor of participating only after undergoing a severe selection process. Blind to the tumult of modern art and buried in their studios, the Academy artists venerated the old masters and ignored any change. But soon, a major event was to upset the laws of representation of shapes and figures—the invention of photography.

The world of the nineteenth century was shaken by major demographic changes and irreversible industrial growth. The ancient rural economic balance disappeared. The captains of industry, exploiting the new technology, built factories to produce more goods faster, supplying an expanding market. It was the triumph of urbanization. Progress brought gas lighting, sewer systems, and running water. Mass transportation was introduced, first with electric streetcars followed by the subway. The cities organized themselves around new hierarchies. Speculators forced artisans and workers from the center of the city to unhealthy outskirts, near the factories. The *nouveaux riches* replaced them—civil servants, merchants, stockholders, bourgeois. The symbols of this new opulence were borrowed from the past. Banks, opera houses, and stock markets were decorated with columns that had an antique look. Steam engines were the foundation of the empire. The industrial aesthetic did not yet exist, nor did modern art.

The Flowers of Evil

The *Belle Époque* was a frivolous time. The great capitals, London, Berlin, New York, and especially Paris, were scenes of flashy, magical celebrations. In Paris, Baron Haussmann, Napoleon III's architect, destroyed the narrow streets in the heart of the city in order to impose a new urban vision. It was the Paris of the Champs-Élysées, Faubourg Saint-Germain, the Bois de Boulogne, the world of the dandies, outdoor terraces, racetracks, public parks, operas, ballets—a permanent spectacle. Flowers were given on every occasion—before dining out, before leaving a café-concert, at the racetrack, or at a street fair. In the theater, where vaudeville triumphed, the bourgeois yearned for stories of illicit love affairs. But this society of luxury and voluptuousness fed on poverty. In the shadow of the City of Light, lived the "little people": rag pickers, waiters, laundresses, milliners, shopgirls, living in their urban hell. The French poet Charles Baudelaire picked his *Flowers of Evil*, identifying with this sad humanity and revealing his painful disillusionment.

Colorful Bouquets

Driven by the need to express in a different way this phenomenon of modern turbulence, the avant-garde artists left objectivity to the photographers, preferring to explore the roads of the senses. They fled the confining studios of the Academy to go directly "to the subject." As the Romans and the Dutch had done before them, these city children turned to nature for renewal, delivered for the first time in the history of Western art, from the heavy burden of representing the world. They were irreparably banned from official competitions. The choice of the jury and the protest generated forced Napoleon III in 1863 to authorize the holding of a parallel exhibition, known as the Salon of the Rejected. Edouard Manet's *Déjeuner sur l'Herbe (Luncheon on the Grass)*, triggered an incredibly violent debate because of its "shamelessness" and "outrageous execution."

In 1874 a group of artists organized a free exhibition in the former studios of the photographer Nadar in Paris. Berthe Morisot, Claude Monet, Pierre-Auguste Renoir, Camille Pissarro, Edgar Degas, Paul Cézanne, and Alfred Sisley showed stunned Parisians their vision of painting.

In comparison to the grandiloquent neoclassicism, their seemingly benign subjects—faces, country meadows, or simple bouquets—were revolutionary. They had observed that black did not exist in nature and that shadows were rich in variations in color. They discovered that the colors of objects changed according to the environment, especially water and snow. The artists created depth by contrasting complementary colors. They proceeded by preserving the purity of each nuance, letting the eye of the viewer carefully rearrange the general harmony, everything vibrating from light (flowers were ideal for the avant-garde's chromatic experiments). They rejected the use of line and contours. Their brush strokes were fluid, liberated from the constraints of realistic *chiaroscuro*; their perspective was off-center and dynamic, the tonalities fresh and luminescent. This freedom, this incomplete expression, profoundly shocked the artists' contemporaries. The critics raged against them. The journalist Louis Leroy, in a sarcastic article, blasted a painting by Monet and its title *Impression,*

Soleil Levant (Impression, Sunrise), which became the insulting name "Impressionist." Faced with the hostility of the established order and public apathy, the Impressionists fought back, organizing other exhibitions. They were encouraged by some discerning intellectuals who understood the importance of their innovations, such as Edmond Duranty, Emile Zola, Zacharie Astruc, and Charles Baudelaire.

Vilified by the critics, ignored by the public, the Impressionists experienced great difficulties in order to survive through their art. In 1886 their eighth exhibition was to be the last. Manet died at the age of 50 without knowing the official glory that awaited him. Sisely ended up poor and resigned. Only Monet and Renoir knew success, and only at the twilight of their careers. The dawn of the twentieth century saw the birth of the last artistic movement that inspired floral collections. Called "l'Art Nouveau," it drew its forms from nature in order to create elegant spaces in a human dimension. In Paris, the

Tulip (*Tulipa*)

subway entrances blossomed like corollas. A mysterious organic life appeared on chairs, lamps, mosaics, and stained-glass windows. Vines coiled around supporting columns of buildings, making use of the architectural qualities of the metal.

The Modern Explosion

From then on, artistic revolutions multiplied at a frenzied pace. The explosion of trends resulted in the affirmation of individual personalities. Historians would later call it contemporary eclecticism. The Dutch painter, Vincent Van Gogh, celebrated the flowers of Provence like no other artist before him, bringing out all the violent colors they sometimes displayed. Flowers played an important role in Henri Matisse's work and life. On his canvases, the twists and turns of the plant's elements are intertwined with those of Oriental fabrics and the liveliness of petals with sun-kissed, flat tints. Flowers also formed a mad whirl in a number of Fauvist works, such as those of Rouault, Vlaminck, and Soutine. Simple and meager bouquets attained a mystic elevation in Odilon Redon's work, emerging from the powdered depths of his pastels. Henry Fantin-Latour's roses

brought him fame and worldly success. The Expressionists Kokoschka, Munch, and Nolde brought violent colors to their extreme. Closer to our time, Giorgio Morandi delicately placed in the center of his paintings a few faded bouquets tinged with infinite nostalgia. Meanwhile, Georgia O'Keeffe pushed to the extreme indiscreet studies of the voluptuous intimacy of smooth corollas. Paradoxically, the classic beauty of bouquets was reborn in the photography of the masters of black and white: André Kertész, Edward Weston, Imogen Cunningham, Karl Blosfeldt, and Robert Mapplethorpe.

The End of Bouquets?

In spite of the turbulent styles that shook the end of the twentieth century, the symbolic meaning of flowers did not evolve a great deal. "Peace and Love" and "Flower Power" were slogans of the youth revolt of the 1960s and 1970s. Nothing new was added, but the influence of religion dimmed. Like all luxury products, flowers are part of the cycle of mass consumption, trivialized but democratized. The rose in the fist of the Socialist parties bears witness to this evolution.

If there are no longer new territories to discover, at least varieties of plants have not yet reached their limit. Every day, new species are born or are being adapted to human use in laboratories. In tropical forests, thousands of plants are waiting to be discovered for their medicinal and nutritive properties. Some have already disappeared, victims of disturbed ecosystems. The particular technique of painting flowers, which originated in Holland in the seventeenth century as a separate pictorial genre and was magnified by the Impressionists, is no longer practiced today. However, flowers have maintained their full expressive power. Recent ecological concerns have brought a contemporary generation of artists closer to nature. And today, bouquets (or other ways of arranging flowers, such as in photographs, displays, and living sculptures) are considered works of art.

The following pages pay vibrant homage to the masters of the past. We used their paintings as models to create with real flowers, arrangements borrowed from their genius. We want to share this pleasure by providing the reader with the means to recreate in the corner of a living room or on a windowsill, one of Jan Davidsz de Heem's baroque compositions, one of Vincent Van Gogh's most celebrated bouquets of sunflowers, or a subtle harmony borrowed from Claude Monet. With this book we hope that their memory will live in your bouquets.

Ten-week stock (*Matthiola*)

Although the works of the first magicians of trompe l'oeil are mostly unknown, their prestige was immense. For example, the reputation of the ancient Greek Zeuxis remains, although there is no trace of his work. According to Pliny the Elder, even the birds were deceived by his talent and tried to pick the grapes he painted on theater curtains.

With infinite patience, the artist has minutely juxtaposed small pieces of glass, choosing each piece with care as touches of color in order to compose shading tones, to draw the contours, giving an illusion of volume. Flowers bloom on a plain, black background; a full-blossomed rose slowly bends its heavy petals; next to it, a peony displays its whiteness, the vine extends its tendrils; and the viewer discerns some carnations, pansies, violets, anemones, clematis, sweet peas, and lilacs. This Roman basket is strikingly similar to the Dutch still lifes of the sixteenth and seventeenth centuries. The resemblance is not accidental, as the Roman patricians and the Dutch bourgeois shared the same passion for realism, the same taste for luxury and money, the same conquering spirit. Religious ceremonies, funerals, and banquets were marked by an abundance of flowers. They were imported in large quantities from Libya, Spain, Persia, Egypt, and Syria, or produced locally, through a combination of heated greenhouses, a network of aqueducts, and the concentrated efforts of gardeners. Conquering warriors and statues of divinities were crowned according to a custom that progressively spread throughout society. The ancient temples were not painted stark white, as they are often represented to us today. They were multicolored, flowered, and perfumed. The wreaths and garlands were composed of flowers, of flowering branches (orange trees, lime trees, almond trees, quince trees, and pomegranate trees), of foliage (laurel, vine, sage, rosemary, olive, ivy, oak), and various conifer branches.

Rose "Frisco" (*Rosa "Frisco"*)

An Anonymous
Roman Artist

SECOND CENTURY

A Flower Basket

Mosaic
Vatican, Pio Clementino Museum

Second
century

The Romans' compositions can be seen as jewelry boxes for roses, their favorite flower. Weave the branches into the shape of a wreath or garland and secure them with iron wire before attaching the flowers. You can use metal supports sold by florists or in flower supply stores. Or you can make them yourself by assembling wire netting from a roll of concentric iron wire. You can also add some blocks of artificial moss that have been soaked in water. Make a slanted cut in the tip of the flower stems and immerse them in deep, tepid water. Add a preservative from the florist or prepare one yourself. *Let them soak several hours before arranging them.

Celosia (*Celosia*)

Page 33

Flowers
• Rose (*Rosa* of all species)
• Hypericum (*Hypericum*)
• Soft Alchemilla (*Alchimilla mollis*)

Leaves
• Ivy (*Hedera*)
• Viburnum with blue berries (*Viburnum*)
• Hops (*Humulus lupulus*)
• Olive tree branches, braided in a crown (*Olea europaea*)

Fruit
• Grapes (*Vitis vinifera*)

Season
• August to October

*Mix one teaspoon chlorine bleach, one tablespoon bottled lemon juice, and one tablespoon sugar in one gallon (3.8 liters) of warm water.

Amaranth (*Amaranthus*)

Flowers
• Rose (*Rosa* of all species)

Leaves
• Ivy *(Hedera)*
• Hops *(Humulus lupulus)*
• Entwined olive tree branches, braided in a crown

Season
• September

Oak leaf (*Quercus*)

Undoubtedly, Pieter Breughel the Elder's second, and most gifted, son, Jan, was the most famous floral painter of the Renaissance. It was a genre to which he brought his soft palette, a brilliant technique, and most of all, a serious scientific concern. Jan Breughel visited botanical gardens in order to better observe rare plants. It sometimes took him an entire year to put together the most beautiful and richest flowers in a single complete bouquet.

Like a well-ordered household, this bouquet is organized in a precise hierarchy. The place of honor, on the upper right, is reserved for an imperial crown *(Fritillaria imperialis)* perched on top of its long, stiff stem. The clear and lively rosy tint of this exceptional flower stands out on the dark background. It forms an elegant and refined pair with the immaculate lily *(Lilium pomponium)* that sits enthroned at its sides. The other important members of the family affectionately surround them: a magnificent full-bloomed peony *(Paeonia)*, some rare tulips, a pair of delicate irises *(Iris germanica)*, a snowball *(Viburnum plicatum)*, and various other roses, daffodils, jonquils, and columbines. A woven tangle of leaves between the petals enhances their delicate colors. The lesser flowers form a procession—wildflowers, hollyhocks, fritillaria, blue nigel-las, small violets, carnations, and primroses. Everything rests on the solid foundation of a wide vase with a classic design. Each species is shown at its best angle; the flowers are depicted with extreme care, perfectly recognizable, the entire picture resembling a herbarium. The final effect appears a bit forced, very frontal, similar to the *millefleurs* medieval tapestries. In spite of the care and minute detail used by Breughel to reproduce the forms and textures, this "cathedral of flowers" remains completely unrealistic, as the varieties of flowers that make up the painting do not bloom at the same time of year. Such an extravagance would be possible only in an idyllic garden that does not exist on earth. In truth, this bouquet is an escapee from paradise.

Tulip "Aladdin" (*Tulipa* "Aladdin")

Jan Breughel

1568 · 1625

Vase Decorated with Flowers

Antwerp,
Royal Museum of Fine Arts

Although today horticultural techniques and the growth of a world market make a wide range of choices available almost all year round, it is difficult to match the richness of Breughel's bouquets, for financial reasons, among other things. Limit your choices to a dozen varieties, and the result will be impressive. Begin by placing the large flower heads at the heart of the bouquet, then arrange the other flowers according to your taste. Make a slanted cut on the ends of the stems of the flowers and immerse them in deep, tepid water, adding a preservative from the florist or your own (see page 34|35). Let them soak several hours before assembling the bouquet. Put a flame at the ends of the stems of the poppies to seal them. Scald the ends of the euphorbia for a few minutes.

Pages 38–39

Flowers
• Tulip (All varieties of *Tulipa*, for example, "Rembrandt" and "Perroquet")
• Poppy *(Papaver)*
• Anemone *(Anemone)*
• Fennel *(Foeniculum vulgare)*
• Iris *(Iris)*
• Gloriosa *(Gloriosa superba)*
• Jasmine *(Jasminum)*
• Euphorbia *(Euphorbia)*
• Sandersonia *(Sandersonia)*
• Crocosmia *(Crocosmia)*

Leaves
• Leaves of flowers

Season
• May to August

Decor
• Chinese porcelain vase; pot in a neoclassic design; marble bowl; antique metal urn or imitation; preferred place in a recessed alcove or in front of a dark drapery at eye level.

Page 41

Flowers
• Rose (*Rosa* of every variety)
• Euphorbia *(Euphorbia)*
• Soft Alchemilla *(Alchemilla mollis)*
• Ten-week stock *(Matthiola)*
• Asclepias *(Asclepias)*
• Snapdragon *(Antirrhinum)*

Leaves
• Leaves of flowers
• Grasses

Season
• June to August

Decor
• Simple tin, copper, or even wood pot, preferably antique (in this case, place a watertight receptacle into it, well supported with blocks of moss, wood, or balls of crumpled newspaper). Place the pot on a dark or even black background.

Euphorbia (*Euphorbia*)

Trained in Utrecht in his father's studio, and later established on his own in Antwerp in 1636, Jan Davidsz de Heem joined together the two great classical traditions of Dutch and Flemish still life. His baroque style is a judicious balance of many decorative effects, enhanced by an astonishing virtuosity and an extremely refined sense of composition. His many imitators were never really able to copy his technical prowess.

This bouquet seems like a ruffled hairdo with its flowers flowing like strands of hair tossed in the wind. One overripe poppy peony is twisted, its brilliant head resting on the marble pedestal, while its dazzling white counterpart raises itself up proudly at the end of its stem. Between these two extremes, a diagonal is drawn that emphasizes the electric-striped markings of stalks of wheat. Three striped tulips and a snowball set up a solid horizontal line, stabilizing the bouquet, revealing its subtle construction. Around these are placed other flowers: blue bindweed, poppies, dappled fritillaria, blue German Irises, wild hyacinths, milfoils, sweet peas with their heavy pods, dimorphic roses, and primroses. It is a collection of wildflowers that ennobles the presence of a few precious flowers. In this lush bouquet, other actors play their parts; a caterpillar wanders around, several butterflies play hide-and-seek, a lizard is hiding in the shade, some ants and a wasp appear, and two snails, their heads exposed, move forward slowly. The budding flowers and the swelling pods of the peas ready to germinate, are a promise for tomorrow. New flowers will replace those that will soon die. In the meantime, the transparent vase filled with limpid water reflects the latticework of a window and a corner of blue sky. A glimpse of light calls us outside, far from our everyday life.

Liatris (*Liatris*)

Jan Davidsz de Heem

1606 · 1684

Still Life with Flowers

Washington,
National Gallery of Art

1 6 4 5

These bouquets can reach impressive heights (spanning more than six feet [2m]). If necessary, use a support made of metal wire or wire netting and blocks of artificial moss to sustain the composition and compensate for the uneven height of the stems. Hide this support in the receptacle (if it is opaque) or with leaves. Also, make sure that sturdy vases are used or, if need be, fill them with sufficient counterweights. Place them at eye level, on a pedestal, if necessary.

Make a slanted cut on the ends of the stems and immerse them in deep, tepid water, adding a preservative (see page 34|35) several hours before assembling them into a bouquet. Prune the ends of the stems by removing the lower leaves. Place the bouquet in a cool room away from drafts. Some bouquets are mainly composed of fruits and vegetables, like the Dutch still lifes from the same period.

Page 45

Flowers
- Peony *(Paeonia)*
- Campanula *(Campanula)*
- Soft Alchemilla *(Alchemilla mollis)*
- Nigella *(Nigella)*
- Delphinium *(Delphinium)*
- Allium *(Allium)*
- Sweet Pea *(Lathyrus odoratus)*
- Carnation *(Dianthus)*
- Astrantia *(Astrantia)*

Leaves
- Leaves of flowers

Season
- May and June

Decor
- Chinese porcelain vase or clear crystal vase, round and rather large; dark background.

Page 47

Flowers
- Pansies *(Viola tricolor)*

Leaves
- Atriplex sorrel
- Hops *(Humulus lupulus)*
- Heather *(Calluna vulgaris)*
- Purple beech *(Fagus sylvatica purpurea)*
- Crocosmia fruit *(Crocosmia)*

Fruits and vegetables
- Artichokes *(Cynara scolymus)*
- Peppers *(Capiscum)*
- Grapes *(Vitis vinifera)*
- Eggplants *(Solanum melongena)*

Season
- August and September

Decor
- Oriental porcelain or crystal vase placed in an alcove or against a dark background.

Pages 48–49

Flowers
- Rose *(Rosa* of every kind; mix the budding flowers with flowers in full bloom)
- Volubilis *(Ipomaea purpurea)*
- Honeysuckle *(Lonicera)*
- Viburnum *(Viburnum)*

Leaves
- Leaves of flowers
- Fennel *(Foeniculum dulce)*

Fruits and vegetables
- Curled lettuce *(Lactua sativa)*
- Grapes *(Vitis vinifera)*
- Cultivated apples *(Malus domestica)*
- Pears *(Pyrus communis)*
- Peaches *(Prunus persica)*
- Sour apples *(Cucurbita pepo)*
- Fennel *(Foeniculum vulgare)*

Season
- August, September

Decor
Transparent or porcelain vase; place before a dark drape or a tapestry.

"Parakeet" Tulip (*Tulipa* "Perroquet")

Pink carnation (*Dianthus*)

Leaving Belgium, Pierre-Joseph Redouté, an itinerant painter, settled in Paris in 1782. His watercolors brought him fame and fortune. Employed at The Royal Jardin des Plantes, which was converted after the revolution into a museum of natural history, Redouté adapted to both political regimes with equal success. His papers recorded the progress of botany; the most beautiful of them were dedicated to roses and to magnificent collections of flowers.

Here is a seemingly modest and transparent illustration with dewdrops sprinkling the jagged leaves. Some roses stand out clearly against the neutral background. This is an illustration of natural history, designed for botanists—the artist scrupulously analyzing each element of the flower, the veins of leaves, the disposition of the petals. We see the distinction between the Yellow Rose and the Bengal Rose (*Rosa lutea* and *Rosa indica*). Ever since roses have become fashionable, horticulturists have created so many new types of roses by hybridization that it has become necessary to continuously update the repertoire. Of interest also were new and little known plants, such as *Amarillys* "Joséphine," *Cactus grandiflorus*, *Redutea heterophylla*, and *Mimulus luteus*. Pierre-Joseph Redouté excelled in objective rep-

resentation. He enriched his precise observations with a play of shadow and light, with watercolored transparencies that earned him praise as the "Raphaël of the Flowers."

His printed collections were widely circulated through naturalistic circles and influenced the taste of the period. Weavers, goldsmiths, carvers, jewelers, and fan makers adapted his models to their decorations. But the outward objective harbored a hidden message. Each rose, from the hermetically sealed bud to the flower in full bloom, showed a different stage of the blossoming. The cycle revealed the dial of a clock, which irreversibly counted off the seasons, emphasizing the ephemeral essence of roses and of life. Time will conquer all, even the truth of science.

Rose "Tiara" (*Rosa* "Diadème")

Pierre-Joseph Redouté

1759 · 1840

Plate from the book
Les Roses de Thory, Rosa Mundi, vol. I

London, Victoria and Albert Museum

Of the hundreds of varieties of roses illustrated by Pierre-Joseph Redouté, very few exist today. Horticulturists prefer to create new varieties rather than perpetuate old ones. However, every beautiful flower taken alone pays tribute to the extraordinary watercolorist. Take your finest pen and inscribe a label that specifies the variety you choose.

Page 53

Flowers
• Rose (*Rosa* "Crystal Palace," or any other beautiful rose)

Leaves
• Leaves of flowers

Season
• May and June

Decor
• A rather small, narrow, and transparent vase; clear background.

Page 55

Flowers
• Iris *(Iris)*
• Rudbeckia *(Rudbeckia)*

Leaves
• Leaves of flowers

Season
• Summer

Decor
• Place the flowers on a sheet of paper or parchment, after having cut the tips of the stems. Immerse them in deep, tepid water, adding a preservative (see page 34|35).

"Tiara" Rose (*Rosa* "Diadème")

Crystal Palace

Protea (*Protea*)

During the middle of the nineteenth century, when Japan emerged from two centuries of total isolation, Europe discovered new textures, flavors, forms, and fragrances. With "Orientalism" came the prints of Hokusai, Utamaro, and Hiroshige. Their living colors, their off-center perspective—the opposite of classic symmetry—the elegance of the line, the subject taken from daily life, all attracted artists who were looking for a new direction.

Wisterias, roses, viburnum, and peonies mix their fragrances—tender nuances in waves. These young Asian women walk together, in an embrace, talking in the moonlight. If there is a constant feature, it is the association between flowers and femininity. No one has ever equaled the finesse of the Japanese artists who linked them in colors. Hokusai explained, "This tone, called the tone of smile, *Wara-ôigouma,* is used on women's faces in order to give them the tint of life, and is also employed for the coloring of flowers." This horizontal scroll *(e-makimono)* must be unwound progressively and examined slowly. A poem, born from the same brush, is featured on the drawing. The painted flowers seem to appear as if by magic on the silk; they float in a space void of signs.

Contrary to European artists, the Asian painters do not feel the urge to record and reconstruct what is real. They deal in feelings. Art is a state of mind, a dream of flowers: chrysanthemums, magnolias, gardenias, bamboo, azaleas, rhododendrons, forsythias, orchids, hibiscus, camellias, cherry and peach blossoms. The calligraphy is multifaceted; it does not send a finished message. The strength or elegance of the stroke of a brush influences the meaning of the ideogram. Free association develops with the play of the imagination. Art is magic, in tune with the soul. In space, in emptiness, readers (Eastern art is read as much as it is looked at), abandon themselves to their own meditation, finally reaching the reflection of the tao, the *ch'i,* the cosmic spirit that breathes life into everything.

Chrysanthemum (*Chrysanthemum*)

Song Guanbao

CHINA, EARLY EIGHTEENTH CENTURY

Detail from a Silk Scroll

Dublin, Chester Beatty Library

Ikebana reflects a precise philosophy and a way of life that fascinates a number of contemporary artists. The apparent simplicity of the floral compositions rests on strict and complex codes and rules. This aesthetic based on a bare look is in harmony with modern homes. Try two simple compositions that draw their inspiration from "levitating," flowers illustrated in the fragment of the silk scroll shown here.

Pages 58–59

Flowers
•Chrysanthemum (*Chrysanthemum* of all kinds)

Leaves
Leaves of flowers

Season
•Fall and winter

Decor
•The flowers are fixed in "Oasis" (a block of artificial moss that holds water); antique bronze or porcelain vases can also be used; some with long, slender necks are designed to carry a single flowering branch; clear background.

Page 61

Flowers
•Anthurium (*Anthurium*)

Season
•Possibly all year

Decor
•A bowl or a flat basin, white or transparent, placed against a clear background.

Peony "Bowl of Beauty" (*Paeonia* "Bowl of Beauty")

Chrysanthemum (*Chrysanthemum*)

An enlightened and cultivated bourgeois, Manet straddled the official Salons and the bohemian world, attempting the impossible reconciliation of both. "One must be a child of one's times and create what one sees," he said. *The Déjeuner sur l'Herbe* (1862) and *Olympia* (1863) caused great uproars at the Salon des Refusés (Salon of the Rejected). An involuntary leader of the Impressionist revolution, Manet yearned for an official recognition that stubbornly escaped him.

Crowned with blue green leaves, peonies ostentatiously display their flesh pink color. Others, bloodred, barely emerge from the shadow. In the foreground, a flower languishes on a table at the foot of a small varnished pedestal that holds the base of a porcelain vase. At its sides, scattered petals look like a unmade bed. According to the Greeks, peonies moan when they are picked. Like the song of the mermaids, this mournful sound was fatal to those who heard it. This painting evokes, in a troubled manner, sensual pleasure. But the abandonment that this bouquet evokes is no longer scandalous and proud like that of Olympia; it conveys the perfume of regret. Some years later, bedridden after a stroke, Manet created a large number of small paintings: portraits of women friends who had come to cheer him up or of flowers gathered from his garden (white lilies, geraniums, carnations, clematis, dahlias, hybrid tea roses, pale or white *Rosa sempervirens,* and more peonies (*Paeonia lactiflora, P. suffructicosa,* etc.). The vases are simple or transparent, sometimes ordinary, everyday glasses. The modest bouquets, swathed in soft light, stand out against a sober and plain background. Emanating from these compositions is the nostalgia for a time past, that of his youth in Montmartre when illusions were not yet lost. These paintings are among Manet's most beautiful. Renouncing the superfluous, the artist concentrated on the essential, fixing on the canvas his immediate sensations with sure and determined strokes. By doing so, he was the first to grasp the constant mobility of the modern world.

"Magic Orb" Peony (*Paeonia* "Magic Orb")

Edouard Manet

1832 · 1883

1 8 6 4

Vase of Peonies on Small Pedestal

Oil on Canvas
Paris, Musée d'Orsay

The nineteenth century saw a flourishing of small bouquets for every occasion, from outings to social events. They were arranged most often with one or two varieties: small flowers placed around a central blossom. The interplay of the colors was also deliberately simplified.

Page 64

Flowers
• Rose (*Rosa* of many kinds, light colors: pink, white)

Leaves
• Leaves of flowers

Season
• April, June

Decor
• Simple, transparent vases, sometimes a small glass; a pastel background matching the color of the flowers.

Page 65

Flowers
• Light red "Sarah Bernhardt" peonies (*Paeonia* "Sarah Bernhardt")
• Dark red peony "Magic Orb" (*Paeonia* "Magic Orb")

Leaves
• Leaves of flowers

Season
• End of spring and summer

Decor
• A simple vase in an Oriental style; dark background to enhance the light pink of the peonies.

Pages 66–67

Flowers
• Rose (*Rosa* of many varieties, soft colors: yellow, pink, white)
• Astrantia *(Astrantia)*
• Dahlia *(Dahlia)*
• Forget-me-not *(Myosotis)*
• Zinnia *(Zinnia)*

Leaves
• Leaves of flowers
• Grass

Season
• May and June

Decor
• Simple, transparent, glass or crystal vase; dark blue background.

Claude Monet discovered the luminescence of water reflections and the variety of colors outdoors. He felt the need to express this natural truth, vibrant and living, as opposed to academic dogmas. To reach that goal, he invented a new style of painting, using small, rapid strokes to break down the colors. His revolution was mocked and rejected before he achieved well-deserved fame toward the end of his life.

On a round table, with earth colors, a garland of withered flowers makes a funeral wreath. It fits tightly around a vase, or rather a white porcelain jar not unlike that used by druggists. From this rather gloomy combination bursts forth an explosion of flamboyant suns. Inundated with light, joyous fireworks make the entire work radiate. The small touches vibrate in lively movements, reconstructing a warm and colorful harmony. Claude Monet was a good gardener and excellent Orientalist. The choice of chrysanthemums was not accidental; the flower, venerated in China, stood for all earthly blessings (longevity, felicity, fertility, and prosperity); in France, it was the flower of the dead. From East to West, the flower reversed its symbolic meaning, the contrasts reconciling themselves like the yin and yang, life in death, light bursting from the shadow. Monet's life was filled with flowers that he painted as an expert. When he settled in Giverny in 1883, the artist became a gardener, growing flowers as he painted his canvases, modeling nature. He composed one of his major works by organizing beds of hollyhocks, dahlias, irises, Japanese and royal lilies, peonies, Oriental poppies, geraniums, roses in profusion, lilacs, tulips, anemones, morning glories, aubrietias, primroses, pansies, wallflowers, and jonquils. Monet spent his final years contemplating the lilies in his water garden. He dedicated his final, huge canvases to a total and definitive fusion with nature—a world of water, flowers, and colors.

Eupatorium (*Eupatorium*)

Claude Monet

1840 · 1926

Vase with Chrysanthemums

1 8 8 0

Oil on Canvas
Washington, National Gallery of Art, Chester Dale Collection

The Impressionist bouquets are improvised and impulsive. Let yourself be guided by your natural inclinations and your spontaneous taste without seeking to compose, which might sometimes give a somewhat stilted look to your arrangement. Make a slanted cut on the ends of the stems and immerse them in deep, tepid water, adding a preservative (see page 34|35) several hours before assembling the bouquet. This will help to prolong the freshness of the cut flowers. Prune the ends of the stems by removing the lower leaves. Crush the ends of the branches or wood stems in order to facilitate the absorption of water. Leave the bouquet in a cool room away from drafts.

Page 71

Flowers
•Waxweed
•Lilac *(Syringa)*
•Sea lavender *(Limonium)*

Leaves
•Leaves of flowers

Season
•Spring

Decor
•A plain, country receptacle with a form and texture that matches the bouquet, such as an earthenware or terra-cotta pot, or a basket or wooden bucket. (Don't forget to line with a watertight receptacle.) Use a clear background.

Page 72

Flowers
•Sea lavender *(Limonium)*
•Astrianta major *(Astrantia)*
•Viburnum *(Viburnum)*
•White Angelica *(Angelica)*

Leaves
•Leaves of flowers

Season
•August, September

Decor
•A large, braided, wicker basket that can hold a rather large vase; pastel background (from blue to green) matching the colors of the bouquet.

Page 73

Flowers
•Chrysanthemum "Bronze Fairie" ("Bronze Fairie" *chrysanthemum)*

Leaves
•Leaves of flowers

Season
•Usually November, but lately more and more throughout the year.

Decor
•White earthenware pot or jug, decorated with flowers; clear background to highlight the green leaves and the brilliance of the flowers.

A founder of impressionism with Monet, Pissarro, Bazille and others, Renoir never denied his classic training and porcelain decorating, and his time at the École des Beaux-Arts (School of Fine Arts). In 1869, at La Grenouillère-sur-Seine, he spent a season of intense creativity, alongside Monet, but several years later, society portraits and nudes led him to return to classic forms.

An abundance of multicolored chrysanthemums form a pleasant and lush bouquet. The greenery remains subdued and the flowers are carefully placed in order to harmonize a range of colors that goes from white to dark red, while passing though shades of yellow and orange. Some extra flowers are strewn at the foot of the vase. The movement that animates the tablecloth and the background of the composition continues the motion of the petals. Renoir pays tribute to the chrysanthemums without mystery or double meanings. He simply shows the flower of the dead in a joyous and happy light. Monet's longtime companion, Renoir had discovered a new technique of painting, using small brush strokes, as seen in the painting shown.

The two friends worked outdoors together on the same subjects—the reflections of water, changing light, regattas, landscapes, figures, and numerous bouquets. Mixing wildflowers with city flowers, concerned only with color, Renoir rapidly composed bouquets of tulips, poppies, peonies, lilacs, wallflowers, irises, daisies, dahlias, and, especially, roses. It was in Normandy, in a friend's garden, that Renoir discovered and learned to love roses, a passion that became more and more important to him. A pale rose that he particularly loved bears his name today. Some years later, in Provence, he built a house surrounded by a rose garden. From then on, the color rose permeated his work—the color of blooming, fleshy, opulent flowers.

Celosia (*Celosia*)

Pierre-Auguste Renoir

1841 · 1919

Bouquet of Chrysanthemums

Oil on Canvas
Rouen, Museum of Fine Arts

Ca. 1884

Renoir's bouquets are gracefully and naturally improvised. In order to arrange them, let yourself be carried away by the harmony of colors. Make a slanted cut on the ends of the flower stems and immerse them in deep, tepid water, adding a preservative (see page 34|35) several hours before assembling the bouquet. Prune the ends of the stems by removing the lower leaves. Crush the ends of the branches or the stems in order to facilitate the absorption of water. Leave the bouquet in a cool room far away from drafts. Make sure to change the water regularly.

Page 76

Flowers
• Peony *(Paeonia)*
• Campanula *(Campanula)*
• Alchemilla *(Alchemilla)*
• Astrantria major *(Astrantia)*
• Sweet Pea *(Lathyrus oderatus)*

Leaves
• Leaves of flowers
• Grass

Season
• May and June

Decor
• Sandstone pot or jug; the background is in soft contrast with the flowers.

Page 77

Flowers
• Delphinium *(Delphinium)*
• Alstromeria *(Alstroemeria)*
• Begonia *(Begonia)*
• Astrantria major *(Astrantia)*
• Rose *(Rosa)*
• White Angelica *(Angelica)*

Leaves
• Leaves of flowers

Season
• May to September

Decor
• Simple vase made of sandstone, earthenware, or terra-cotta; large woven basket, or wooden bucket lined with a waterproof receptacle; light background.

Page 78

Flowers
• Chrysanthemum *(Chrysanthemum,* in a variety of types and colors)

Leaves
• Leaves of flowers

Season
• Fall

Decor
• A simple terra-cotta pot containing a rather large, waterproof vase; dark, neutral background to highlight the many colors in this bouquet.

Page 79

Flowers
• Delphinium *(Delphinium)*
• Alstromeria *(Alstroemeria)*
• Begonia *(Begonia)*
• Astrantia major *(Astrantia)*
• Rose *(Rosa)*
• White Angelica *(Angelica)*

Leaves
• Leaves of flowers
• Grasses

Season
• May to September

Decor
• Earthenware pot or jug; light background to highlight the green leaves and the brilliance of the flowers.

Vincent Van Gogh's failed career as a missionary, his disappointed love affairs, and the rejection of his family were all put behind him when he arrived in Arles in February, 1898. The shock of his discovery of impressionism in Paris had brightened his palette and the light of southern France transformed it radically. He who had until then ignored flowers, was suddenly fascinated by them and overwhelmed by violent emotions that ultimately proved fatal.

Vincent Van Gogh traveled throughout the countryside as a planter and laborer. The land was his. He buried himself in wheat fields, meadows, orchards, and gardens, absorbing all of nature. His eyes squinting under the bright, hot sun, he immersed himself in the earth's perfumes. When he came home, bowls of fire seemed to dance in his dazzled eyes. He worked frenetically, with a sure touch. The flowers appeared just as he saw them—a dozen thick stars irradiating the canvas with their burning light. In a state of near intoxication, he exalted a luminous hymn— "yellow sun, pale yellow sulfur, pale lemon gold." Van Gogh made the springtime burst with brilliance. But like Icarus, the mythological Greek who flew too close to the sun, the artist burned his wings because of the intense contact.

Irises, roses, carnations, wildflowers, sunflowers, anemones, poppies, wild arum, buttercups, lilacs, branches of acacia, oleander, chestnut trees, almond trees in flower; a forest of pear trees, twisted olive trees, fields of poppies...Van Gogh picked armfuls of flowers. They momentarily relieved the fever that burned him, clearing away the shadows of his world. A humble yet passionate painter, the vigor, if not the violence, of his brush strokes foreshadowed expressionism. Van Gogh personified the solitary artist, misunderstood, ignored, rejected, reduced to perpetually begging for his subsistence. It is bitter irony that today his flowers are the most expensive in the world. On March 30, 1987, the Japanese insurance company Yasuda Fire and Marine paid $50 million for this painting.

Iris (*Iris*)

Vincent Van Gogh

1853 · 1890

Sunflowers (Vase with Twelve Sunflowers)

1889

Oil on Canvas
Private collection

Van Gogh glorified wildflowers, simple pitchers, and the crumbling walls of his room. An inventor of new and extreme harmonies—yellow, violet, green, orange, and blue—color was his only logic. Dare to try strong, even violent, combinations—blue and bright orange, lemon yellow and apple green, violet, white, and sulfur yellow. Do not hesitate to paint the vases. Avoid using frames. Let the flowers spill over and curve naturally.

Make a slanted cut on the ends of the stems and immerse them in deep, tepid water, adding a preservative (see page 34|35) several hours before assembling the bouquet. Prune the lower leaves from the end of the stems. Crush the ends of the branches (of the laurel) or the woody stems in order to facilitate the absorption of water. Place the bouquet in a cool room, away from drafts. Be sure to change the water regularly.

Pages 82–83

Flowers
• Sunflower *(Helianthus annuus)*

Leaves
• Leaves of flowers

Season
• March to October

Decor
• Sandstone or earthenware pot or jug; bright background.

Page 85

Flowers
• Blue tipped Iris *(Iris pogoniris)*

Leaves
• Leaves of flowers

Season
• May to July

Decor
• Very simple pot or jug; acid lemon yellow or green background.

Page 84

Flowers
• Oleander in blossom *(Nerium oleander)*

Leaves
• Leaves of flowers

Season
• May to October

Decor
• Simple, country jug; bright background to contrast with the flowers.

Odilon Redon's strange and enigmatic work translates his fascination for the inner areas of the subconscious that Freud would define a few years later. His vision, which fluctuates between dream and reality, is, at first, unsettling and mysterious. It is expressed by the darkness of his charcoal drawings and etchings. Around 1890, after discovering color through the medium of flowers, his pastels brightened to express optimism.

The bouquet emerges in mysterious levitation from the texture of the paper. It comes from far away, from somewhere deeper than the night, to arrive on the surface at the edges of the frame, a few inches from the observer. The flowers appear to be drawn with their own pollen, an effect that pastels alone can render technically because of their powdery and blurry texture. The colors are unreal, stark, almost too pure; they have the innocence of children astonished at their own existence. "Flowers that came from the joining of two rivers, of representation, and of memory," said the artist. And the French nature poet Francis Jammes "added, [...] they have a charm impossible to grasp, a question, formulated, from these three colors, so childish, so crudely placed that it is their juxtaposition alone that creates the subtlety, the skill, and the

infinite nuance." Odilon Redon did not forget his botanical studies. His knowledge was so great that he no longer had to copy nature, thereby composing bouquets he had envisioned. Master Odilon's herbarium is well stocked: daisies, roses, peonies, cornflowers, geraniums, sunflowers, anemones, lilacs, mimosas, nasturtiums, morning glories, carnations, tulips, and the ever-present poppy, the flower of dreams. Planted in full light, the flowers are haloed with a glowing cloud, the vestige of a voyage to an immense and unknown world. But, upon waking, there is no memory of the nocturnal journey; the secret is well guarded. All that remains is a bit of sand at the corner of the eye, a feeling of melancholy that slowly disappears, a few traces of fragrance of an unknown origin. Dream or nightmare, everything has drifted off to oblivion.

Nigella damascena, Venus Hair (*Nigella damascena*)

Odilon Redon

1840 · 1916

Anemones and Lilacs in a Blue Vase

1909-1916

Paris,
Petit Palais Museum

If you are lucky enough to have a garden, you will be able to create bouquets that pay tribute to Master Odilon. Make a slanted cut on the ends of the stems and immerse them in deep, tepid water, adding a preservative (see page 34|35) several hours before assembling the bouquet. This process preserves the freshness of cut flowers, even those from your garden. If the arrangement seems too full, make a ball of fine wire mesh to stabilize the stems. Hide it in the vase or among the leaves. Prune the ends of the stems by removing the lower leaves. Crush the ends of the branches or woody stems in order to facilitate the absorption of water. Leave the bouquet in a cool room away from drafts. Fill the stems of the herbs with water, then seal them with cotton or wax. Be sure to change the water regularly.

Page 89

Flowers
• Rudbeckia *(Rudbeckia)*
• Zinnia *(Zinnia)*
• Lupine *(Lupinus)*
• Delphinium *(Delphinium)*

Leaves
• Leaves of flowers

Season
• May to July

Decor
• An enamel metal jug, simple but colored; a dark background that goes with the bouquet.

Page 91

Flowers
• Nigella *(Nigella)*
• Zinnia *(Zinnia)*
• Lupine *(Lupinus)*
• Delphinium *(Delphinium)*

Leaves
• Leaves of flowers

Season
• May to July

Decor
• Terra-cotta pot lined with a glass or plastic receptacle; background partially dark to go along with the bouquet.

Veronica (*Veronica*)

Ranuncula buttercup (*Ranunculus acris*)

Snapdragon (*Antirrhinum majus*)

Paul Cézanne partici-pated in the first Impressionist exhibi-tion with dark, vigorous, and thickly painted works from his youth. Waiting im-patiently for success, this irascible man from Provence did not accept criticism well, even from his friend Emile Zola. He iso-lated himself in Aix to slowly forge a solid and mature body of work that was a foun-dation for the art of the twentieth century, "approaching nature through the cylinder, the sphere, and the cone...."

A blue pillar, in the shape of a vase, solidly built, has a veined foliage inlaid with a trowel. The petals and the leaves of the gerani-ums form red, green, and white tiles. The irises are covered with plaster crepis and held up by a scaffolding of cut branches. At the foot of this monu-ment rest three apples with as much weight as roundness. Next to a large inkwell, an oval plate surrounds the vase in order to better support it. The win-dowsill, a wall against which rests a bottle covered with wicker as thick as the table, makes a frame for the central subject. This construction is designed to last, executed with care and patience. The gestures are earthy, the materials solid.

All precautions are obviously necessary as the foundations—the plane of the table—are in dangerous imbalance, ready to tip over. The line of the horizon is uncertain; the vanishing points are already gone. Perspective, that beautiful invention of the Re-naissance, is also gone. The ele-ment that allowed figures and objects to be anchored in a perfectly controlled space was unable to resist progress. Images move fre-netically, endowed with a relentless pho-tographic precision. Distances are made smaller by the new use of gas and elec-tricity. An old world collapses; a new world seeks its own language. Cézanne rein-vented space by shaping it little by little, according to the elements he placed on the canvas, creating a profound area in color and perspective. From the expression of simple forms emerged a space with many points of view.

Cultivated apple (*Malus domestica*)

Paul Cézanne

1839 · 1916

The Blue Vase

1885-1887

Oil on Canvas
Paris, Musée d'Orsay

Use a branch that is stripped and well shaped (willow or olive tree, for example). Place it in the center of the arrangement to support the stems of the flowers. Make a slanted cut on the end of the stems and immerse them in deep, tepid water, adding a preservative (see page 34|35) several hours before assembling the bouquet. Prune the ends of the stems by removing the lower leaves. Crush the ends of the branches or the woody stems in order to facilitate the absorption of water. Leave the bouquet in a cool room, away from drafts. Make sure to change the water regularly.

Page 95

Flowers
- Lisianthus *(Lisianthus)*
- Phlox *(Phlox)*
- Symphorine *(Symphoricarpos)*
- Hortensia *(Hydrangea macrophylla)*
- Rose *(Rosa)*
- Chamomile *(Anthemis)*

Leaves
- Leaves of flowers
- Weeds

Fruit
- Cultivated apples *(Malus domestica)*

Season
- August to September

Decor
- A rather large, white porcelain vase; dark background to contrast with the white of the porcelain and the drapecloth.

Page 96

Flowers
- Tulip *(Tulipa)*

Leaves
- Leaves of flowers

Fruit
- Cultivated apples *(Malus domestica)*

Season
- August to September

Decor
- Tall vase; light background.

Page 97

Flowers
- Delphinium *(Delphinium)*
- Chrysanthemum *(Chrysanthemum)*
- Symphorine *(Symphorincarpos)*
- Veronica *(Veronica)*
- Carnation *(Dianthus)*

Leaves
- Leaves of flowers

Season
- August to September

Decor
- Long transparent or dark vase, with glass marbles on the bottom; light background.

Symphorine (*Symphoricarpos*)

Between the somber palette of the first works of Duconseil's convalescent clerk and the florescence of the great *Blue Nudes,* in bright color, lies Henri Matisse's exemplary career. His solitary explorations—he was part of the Fauvist movement for three short years—led him to an extreme economy of style. With the fortuitous marriage of basic line and a few pure colors, Matisse created interest and happiness.

A vase teeters on a poorly made wooden dresser. A drawer with two knobs, a marble slab, more drawers, and a large oval mirror make an uncertain base for a terra-cotta vase. The irises spring out in a disordered fashion and continue to expand. This imbalance mars the whole scene. Could this uncertain image be the work of a madman? What is the reason behind this work? After the first impact, when the shock dies down, the colors appear fresh and gay, shimmering. Although rarely combined, they are harmonious together. A fine network of arabesques fastens the forms together and keeps them from tipping over. On the left, a spiral of wood is anchored to a petal; on the right, the flower heads grip the frame of a mirror and the vase looks like marble, all according to a well-planned play of forms and counter-forms.

In seeking a new fusion between line and color, Henri Matisse encountered the floral arabesques and feminine curves that he combined constantly. He selected flowers and plants for their color or twisting design, such as pineapples, anemones, palm trees, magnolias, ferns, nasturtiums, lilacs, cyclamens, poppies, geraniums, petunias, arum lilies, narcissus, agaves, fig trees, and, everywhere, philodendron leaves. A lush decor of vases, jugs, pots, plates, rugs, draperies, curtains, fans, cushions, screens—Chinese, Moroccan, or Persian—formed, along with the bouquets, a setting where harem girls held court in quiet meditation.

Garden anemone (*Anemone pavonina*)

Henri Matisse

1869 · 1954

Vase of Irises

Oil on Canvas
Saint Petersburg, Hermitage Museum

Matisse's bouquets are colorful but not multicolored. Limit yourself to two or three contrasting colors; for example, the orange of flame flowers with the violet of a curtain. Supporting structures are not necessary; rather, let the flowers fall naturally. Their curves will blend in with the arabesques of vases and Moroccan fabrics that Matisse loved so much. Make a slanted cut on the end of the stems and immerse them in deep, tepid water, adding a preservative (see page 34|35) several hours before assembling the bouquet. Prune the ends of the branches by removing the lower leaves. Crush the ends of the branches of the woody stems in order to facilitate the absorption of water. Leave the bouquet in a cool room, away from drafts. Make sure to change the water regularly.

Page 101

Flowers
• Flame flower *(Kniphofia)*

Leaves
• Asparagus *(Asparagus)*

Fruit
• Cultivated apples *(Malus domestica)*

Season
• August to September

Decor
• Moroccan vases and cups in various shapes; dark, even black background.

Page 102

Flowers and leaves
• Philodendron *(Philodendron monstera)*

Season
• All year

Page 102

Flowers
• Garden anemone *(Anemone pavonina,* diverse and varied)

Leaves
• Leaves of flowers
• Anthurium *(Anthurium)*

Fruit
• Giant pumpkin *(Cucurbita maxima)*

Season
• Spring to winter

Decor
• Moroccan vase and table-cloth with lacy designs; bright background.

Page 103

Flowers
• Garden anemone *(Anemone pavonia,* diverse and varied)

Leaves
• Leaves of flowers

Fruit
• Cultivated apples *(Malus domestica)*

Season
• Spring to winter

Decor
• Terra-cotta pot; for the background a colored drapery with a graphic pattern.

Some infrequent trips, one exhibition or two, and long, solitary walks, inevitably led Giorgio Morandi back to the center of Bologna, to his room, which was also his office and studio. He created more than 1,500 paintings (and many sketches, watercolors, and drawings), practically without changing his subject or point of view. The poetry of his work and his life fluctuated between the smallest distances.

Small roses, withered and crumpled like balls of scrap paper, have turned dusty. A gray snow reigns over all, drifting in the light, and making colors pale. It has invaded everything, clinging to the sides of a small vase, covering the tables and walls of the room. The solitary bouquet stands in a decor that is too vast; it does not feed our dreams. A mute actor on the scene, it just waits for something or someone. Perhaps it is only waiting for time to pass. But time has stopped, stranded in the evening light. Will the departing day ever end?

In order to ward off boredom, the observer scans the canvas. The surface, painted and repainted, is soft, worn by the caress of the brush. The colors of the oils are spread in several smooth coats; the sinuous waves are like those of a master pastry chef, who is icing a sponge cake.

The colors have a sweet and milky harmony. The flowers are modeled in thick paint. One senses the delicate perfume from their younger days. Time, once again, has stopped, but the insidious anguish has vanished. The small unusual scenes that Giorgio Morandi staged were ruled by a passionate order. He felt that objects had souls. He loved these ordinary boxes or pots he discovered by chance for their wrinkles and their defects, like his brushes, faithful and tired companions that had become worn out. He did not throw them away, but rather, respectfully, buried them in his garden. The objects are reflections of the human mystery. They contain traces of those who made them, their thousands of uses. They are our memory and our history.

Dried rose (Rosa)

Giorgio Morandi

1860 · 1964

Flowers

Milan,
private collection

1921

Giorgio Morandi's minimal poetry requires a great deal of time and patience to reproduce. First, you must rummage through attics and flea markets to find the right pots, boxes, and bottles. Then, paint them by creating a range of related pastel colors. Finally, delicately dry small bunches of roses.

Page 107

Flowers
•Rose (*Rosa,* varieties that lend themselves well to drying, such as the R. "Baccarolla" or the R. "Nicole.")

Leaves
•Leaves of flowers

Season
•All year, depending upon the variety selected

Decor
•Small porcelain vase with elongated neck in pastel tones that can be repainted; the colors of the vase should be chosen to match the tones of the background and the dried flowers.

Page 109

Flowers
•Rose (*Rosa,* varieties that lend themselves well to drying).

Leaves
•Leaves of flowers

Season
•All year, depending upon the variety chosen

Decor
•Small vases, apothecary jars or pitchers, combined with various boxes and elongated bottles; painted uniformly with a brush or spray gun with paint suitable for glass; use pastel and matching tones.

Along with Edward Hopper, Georgia O'Keeffe was one of the first American artists to distance herself from European influences. She was also one of the first women to emerge in an almost exclusively masculine world. She began to paint flowers in 1918, shortly after meeting Edward Stieglitz, the renowned photographer. The majority of her "portraits" of flowers date from that happy period in her life.

A giant iris occupies the total space of the canvas out to the far edges. The eye of the artist is fixed on the flower and transformed into a camera lens, dilating a fragment to the maximum. Through the intervention of the frame, this innocuous detail has become an immense landscape. The petals deepen into valleys; the stamens look like giant baobab trees. This universe is almost uniformly white except for the lively yellow accents and some greenish shadows. The image wavers between abstraction and realism.

The head of the flower—lace flounces and cotton petticoats—reveals to the viewer a completely feminine intimacy. The angelic whiteness is also alluring—an ambivalent image, both modest and indiscreet. It is impossible to guess the format of this picture, so great is the contrast between the actual size of its subject and the huge size of the picture. (In reality, it measures 2 feet 6 inches × 3 feet 3 inches [76.2 × 100 cm]). A startled spectator would say that humans feel like butterflies in front of Georgia O'Keeffe's paintings. When she died, the artist left more than 200 paintings of flowers. Her garden contained irises, zinnias, petunias, sweet peas, roses, poppies, lilies, cactus flowers, camellias, and orchids. The garden was mostly monochromes—white, black, purple, or crimson.

But can one speak in this case of paintings of flowers? From joyous poppies to somber irises, one reads Georgia O'Keeffe's story. Passionate love inspired in her the wild and flamboyant reds; her later flowers were dark and unsettling. She preferred the New Mexico desert landscape, her last refuge. Georgia O'Keeffe's flowers reflect her soul as well as any self-portrait.

Wild pansy (*Viola tricolor*) and forget-me-nots (*Myosotis*)

Georgia O'Keeffe

1887 · 1986

White Iris #7 **1 9 5 7**

Oil on Canvas
Madrid, Thyssen-Bornemisza Foundation

Make miniature montages by mixing petals and large flower heads held by hidden pins or hooks. It should all float on the water of a white, bluish, or transparent bowl or tray.

Page 113

Flowers
•Hollyhock *(Althea)*

Leaves
•Rhododendron *(Rhododendron)*

Season
•Summer

Decor
•Transparent or white bowl or tray.

Page 115

Flowers and leaves
•Cyclamen *(Cyclamen)*

Season
•April to June

Decor
•Bowl or large transparent or white tray.

Arum (*Zantedeschia*)

Eustoma (*Eustoma grandiflorum*)

Arum (*Zantedeschia*)

Bibliography

The Culture of Flowers,
Goody J., Cambridge University Press, 1993.

La Nature morte,
Skira P., Editions d'art Albert Skira, 1989.

*Les Peintres de fleurs en France
de Redouté à Redon,*
Hardouin-Fugier E., Grafe E.,
Les éditions de l'amateur, 1992.

Les Fleurs vues par les peintres,
Bazin G., Edita-La bibliothèque des arts,
1984.

Le Peintre et l'histoire naturelle,
Pinault M., Flammarion, 1990.

A History of Flower Arrangement,
Berrall J. S., London, 1978.

*Dictionnaire des peintres, dessinateurs,
graveurs et sculpteurs,*
Bénézit, Gründ, 1976.

A Book of Flowers,
Casts A., Phaidon, 1973.

Les dernières fleurs de Manet,
Gordon R., Forge A., Hershcher, 1986.

French Flower Painters,
Lamarre C., Wilson, 1989.

European Flower Painters,
Mitchell P., Black, 1973.

*A Dictionary of Flower, Fruit and
Still-Life Painters,*
Pavière S., Lewis, 1962.

*Peintres de fleurs en France du XVIIe
au XIXe siècle,*
Paris, musée du Petit Palais, 1979.

Correspondance complète de Van Gogh,
Van Gogh V., Gallimard/Grasset, 1960.

Ecrits et propos sur l'art,
Henri Matisse, Hermann, 1972.

*La nature morte, de l'Antiquité
au XXe siècle,*
Nouvelle édition révisée, Sterling C.,
Macula, 1985.

Georgia O'Keeffe, One Hundred Flowers,
Callaway N., Alfred A. Knopf, 1990.

The History of Impressionism,
Rewald J., N.Y. Museum of Modern Art,
1961.

Le jardin de Claude Monet,
Truffaut G., Jardinage, novembre 1924.

*Les notes du fourneau Saint-Michel et du
musée de la vie rurale en Wallonie,*
Musée P.-J. Redouté, Edition du départe-
ment enseignement et culture de la prov-
ince du Luxembourg, service des musées
provinciaux luxembourgeois, 1989.

L'Arte moderna,
Argan G.-C., Sansoni, 1970.

Storia dell'arte italiana,
Argan G.-C., Sansoni, 1968.

Anni con Giorgio Morandi,
Raimondi G., Mondadori, 1970.

Odilon Redon,
Cassou J. Planty-Delta-Cluwert, 1972.

L'art du bouquet,
Clairoix N.C., Paris, 1913.

...and other beautiful books published by Barron's:

Garden Flowers
Hertle B., Kiermeier P., Nickig M., 1994.

The Garden of Claude Monet
Prost C., 1995.

Roses
Bunemann O., Becker J., 1994.

Shrubs in the Wild and in Gardens
Kremer B. P., 1995.

Water Gardens
Stadelmann P., 1992.